D0129371

This journal belongs to:

____

Copyright © 2017. All rights reserved.

No part of this book or this book as a whole may be used, reproduced, or transmitted in any form or means without written permission from the publisher.

Table of Contents

Topic/Theme	Page	Topic/Theme	Page

Topic/Theme	Page	Topic/Theme	Page

Topic/Theme	Page	Topic/Theme	Page

Topic/Theme	Page	Topic/Theme	Page

Made in the USA
Coppell, TX
03 January 2021

47458284R00059